I0621992

A Leap Year of Haiku

A
Leap
Year
of
Haiku

A Leap Year of Haiku

Michael R. Lane

BARE BONES PRESS
P.O. Box 9653, Seattle, WA 98109

Published by Bare Bones Press

Printed on acid-free paper.

Design: Bare Bones Press, LLC
Production: Bare Bones Press.com
Cover Art: Michael R. Lane

Bare Bones Press, LLC
P.O. Box 9653
Seattle, WA 981909

www.michaelrlane.com
www.barebonespress.com

First Edition: November 2023

To Persistence, Hope and Faith

1

one thousand years in
the body of nature is
a flitting heartbeat.

2

evening does not fall
it drifts and floats and settles
as cool perfumed mist.

3

clear water boiling
eggs in copper bottom pot
rattle the steel lid.

4

a split package of
pink hotdogs broiled on asphalt
blistered by the sun.

5

robust woman plopped
down in upholstered bus seat
released grateful sigh.

6

straw liquid entrails
from a center crushed beer can
stained a dust gray street.

7

tow truck towing car
broken down by the roadside
awaits assistance.

8

most people are like
water they travel the path
of least resistance.

9

I sink into her
skin like soft down pillows on
satin cotton clouds.

10

suitcase weighed with past
burdens stitched together by
erratic futures.

11

a town so small when
a child is born residents
shoot off fireworks.

12

through plumes of black smoke
emerged his savior
clothed in ocean, land and sky.

13

crisp snaps of green beans
shot reality TV
of rapt spectator.

14

we shield ourselves with
masks and gloves hoping to foil
a virus killer.

15

winter stifled growth
and scents and the stretch of life
forced hibernation.

16
spring liberated
winter baroness from her
ice castle prison.

17
a child in swim trunks
damp towel draped over bare shoulder
walks with grandmother.

18
cool July morning
homeless rummage castoffs
for scraps to survive.

19
hills of Magnolia
across greens of Interbay
clear resident view.

20
abandoned school bus
homeless children forlornly
ate their free school lunches.

21
coronavirus
pandemic oppressor of
free society.

22
he popped a cherry
Lifesaver into his mouth.
"Sugar shot," he said.

23
his placid mind flipped
through commemorative leafs
of chance memories.

24
a drunken mailman
threw mail on the open porch
scattered dispatches.

25
why are funerals
private moments of grief put
on public display?

26
greed rules that is why
all I expect out of a
job is a paycheck.

27
the bus driver said
"Amtrak" but it sounded more
like the word anthrax.

28
a friend asked if I
dreamed. "Yes, of course," I said while
asleep and awake.

29
corporations are
capital gods. big business
is the messiah.

30
chaos sires demon
seeds nurtured in hostile soil
sprouting anarchy.

31
my friend night dampens
light tempering edict sight
freeing four senses.

32
for profit prisons
supply and demand humans
for legal tender.

33
selfish leaders rot
fabric of society
leaving fungus spores.

34
I find it easy
to social distance myself
from other people.

35
mirror crack ratchets
its crooked way through the path
of my loneliness.

36
black Americans
judged by twelve persons who are
not jury of peers.

37
you can give anyone
carpenter tools. that does not
make a carpenter.

38
introverts under-
stand extroverts. the reverse
is not always true.

39
gray morning light beads
within soft morning raindrops
cleansing urban world.

40
the planet is worth
saving. the same cannot be
said of humankind.

41

protesting a grand
cause. destruction fatal flaw
to freedom of speech.

42

private prisons are
modern penal colonies
without oversight.

43

cops' knees on black necks
preserving ingrained system
of fixed tyranny.

44

COVID-19 death
sentence president willing
to sharpen the axe.

45

injustice fueled rage
ignited by another
ruthless cop murder.

46
dark clouds billowing
lightning veins between them
brain stem of the skies.

47
contagious lethal
virus pandemic outbreak
strangles populace.

48
family is not
born into blood relatives
that bond is proven.

49
pencil sketches shape
delicate outlines of her
sensuous body.

50
institutional
racism embeds roots of
social injustice.

51
conservationists
gallantly serve humankind
deserve more respect.

52
ozone layer to
third sun planet stratosphere
protective membrane.

53
gray mist crowns mountain
ranges merge with hazy sky
pines kiss goodbye.

54
unnatural deaths
plague black men like pus filled boils
in America.

55
rage fuels vengeful wrath
incinerating hope and
tranquil hearts and souls.

56
smog glazed high noon sun
center of solar system
radiating life.

57
dip your nib into
the inkwell of raven ink
pen your destiny.

58
fragile human souls
body battered existence
spiritual journey.

59
thick ash colored smoke
billows and corkscrews into
docile atmosphere.

60
jealousy has a
bitter and acidic voice
bent on destruction.

61
youthful memories
bolster the past but tend to
strangle the future.

62
when you grow up in
the bedrock of racism
nothing surprises you.

63
can't change people's minds
hearts or beliefs unless they
are ready for change.

64
our pious species
devours God's creation in
order to survive.

65
fractured egos stunt
fragile progress engaging
immoral tyrants.

66

sunlight from blue skies
illuminate varying
urban scenery.

67

sweat rolls down the nape
of her slender neck like tears
knifing her wing blades.

68

when sunlight kisses
the land, are they lewd lovers
or intimate friends?

69

phantoms haunt night dreams
claw at subconscious fibers
seeking where to roost.

70

heat rises toward night
embracing a starlit sky
crowned by the moon.

71
the universe is
indifferent to our wants,
needs and desires.

72
thick gray fog tumbles
from mountain tops caressing
all it encounters.

73
yellow sun holds court
sovereign received by earth's
native disciples.

74
the rusty heel of
bigotry is spiked and stained
with innocent blood.

75
Floyd, Ahmaud, Taylor,
targets charged with being black
sanctioned blue killers.

76
black lives that matter
extinguished in their prime as
a sadistic curse.

77
peaceful protesters
treated as nation foes they
attempt to uplift.

78
Summer Taylor killed
run down by car driven by
Dawit Kelete.

79
bright color arcs tinge
both sides of our center sphere
sun dog standing guard.

80
flooding emotion
iron ore its pulsing core
solidifies love.

81
money is not the
root of all evil it does
exhume human greed.

82
presumptions and kin
assumptions are quicker than
reason to unfold.

83
a cawing crow pecks
at the fresh entrails of a
road-killed gray squirrel.

84
pure echoing chimes
birthing from the peaceful womb
of serenity.

85
past memory fixed
future born of wings to fly
present inhales now.

86
wonder eclipses
rational when it comes to
all exploration.

87
eternal gratitude
for those courageous persons
battling injustice.

88
cawing, chirping, breezes
rustling leaves, seagulls' cries spread
sunlit morning songs.

89
nation in turmoil
narcissistic autocrat
deludes populists.

90
goodwill manifest
from overwhelming demand by
unyielding forces.

91

I coax love as if
it were a picky eater
snubbing healthy foods.

92

fetid acrimony
breathes and digest rancid bile
rearing jealous grist.

93

cellphone appendage
to some, cellular leash to
others, phone to me.

94

when she kisses me
time ceases, stills, awaiting
our tender release.

95

callus fingertips
trace her scented bare shoulders
soft skin, satin touch.

96

I can hear fifteenth
avenue west traffic flow,
sounds like ocean waves.

97

home, stress free refuge,
residence to live and dream,
escape from the din.

98

incredulous thoughts
irritate trust like starved fleas
feasting on warm blood.

99

loneliness beckons,
"Let's spend some time together,"
backs away then leaves.

100

words expose themselves
language symbols form in mind
dance across the page.

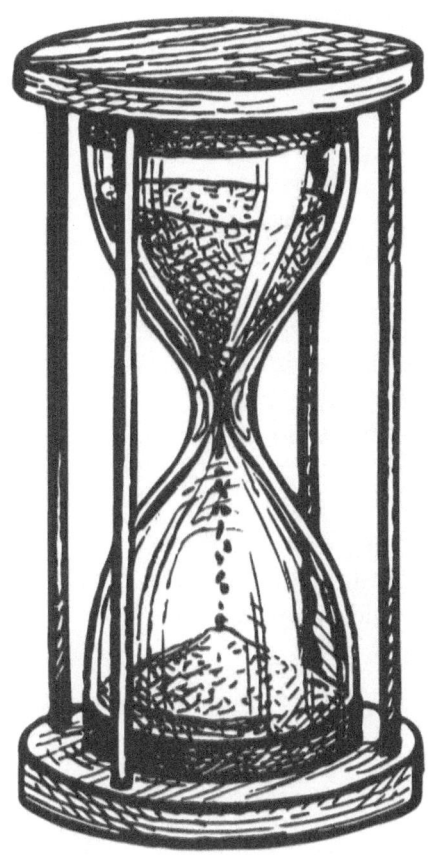

101

arrogant humans
worldwide infestation stock
destruction and waste.

102

white-collar sweatshops
continue tradition of
exploiting labor.

103

human labor a
universally oppressed
subjugated force.

104

doing what is right
opposed to what is selfish
should be our nature.

105

imperialist
president garners support
to abuse power.

106
living wages for
manual workers are as
rare as finding gold.

107
harbinger of light
wade us through stifling darkness
of quicksand and blight.

108
exploitation of
workers a perennial
worldwide pandemic.

109
moral fortitude
stalwart mental resolve stem
from ceaseless courage.

110
unreasonable
judgement pollutes bias minds
like contaminates.

MICHAEL R. LANE

111
prejudice sparks race
fires incinerating hopes,
legal rights and claims.

112
conservatism boast
status quo dogma averse
to relevant change.

113
a person spitting
garbled patriotic words
contributes nothing.

114
some people are born
voracious parasites bent
on self-indulgence.

115
morning calm settles
like warm dew seeping into
my curious soul.

116
dawn whispers its call
for sun to begin our day
in glory or sin.

117
papier-mache people
doused in ripened truth serum
crumple and slink away.

118
upon a cloud drifts
Serenity kissing Peace
goading Love to smile.

119
convictions require
stringent focus commitment
on staunch principles.

120
my natural state
is silence nourishing me
with tacit rations.

121
adrift in reading
basking in literature
is my paradise.

122
left my key in my
mailbox kind neighbor left note
where I could find it.

123
hot summer days make
muggy indoor stays during
virus quarantine.

124
liberated minds
leap, soar, bank, dive, skimming
alien oceans.

125
quiet of morning
greets me in its welcoming
golden arms of dawn.

126
a teakettle's piercing
whistle alerts time for my
aromatic brew.

127
music echoes through
perpetual harmonies
of sound and silence.

128
sovereignty marries
anarchy lethal lovers
anchored by warped faiths.

129
federal shock troops
invade democratic camps
incite violence.

130
fascism vermin
drain democratic body
of freedom lifeblood.

131
Negro, Colored, black,
African American,
bottom line human.

132
should fascism win
2020 USA
who will celebrate?

133
Portland, Oregon
constitutional test site
for despot regime.

134
path of deception
is as crooked as a snake's
slithering journey.

135
writing bouquet of
inklings pollinate fertile
imagination.

136
sunrise and sunset
implacable rituals
of nature's cycle.

137
autocrats promote
oligarchy masquerades
as law and order.

138
fragile countenance
of bright face democracy
scarred, bruised and bloodied.

139
noisy vacuum
arouses tired gray carpet
sucking fabric clean.

140
peeler skims away
cucumber skin like skaters
gliding on smooth ice.

141
devaluation
of art dilutes our vision
cremates our passion.

142
ignorant people
disparage intelligence
reproach book learning.

143
faith can motivate
one to action, courage will
prolong your resolve.

144
vampires walk amongst
us not only at night but
in the light of day.

145
evil principles
rooted in parables of
sin eludes truth light.

146
hope embraces faith
twin hearts sharing beliefs in
a haven of peace.

147
irrevocably
yearning for something forever
lost and buried, time.

148
conversation needs
listening and respect in
order to be real.

149
armed militias
oppressors camouflaged as
loyal patriots.

150
stuck a straight pin
through the eye of a needle
to see if I could.

151
cool still gray morning
settles my rampant thinking
like fog on a bay.

152
diplomacy the
art of verbal seduction
in hostile climates.

153
unity is the
solvent that could cleanse many
societal ills.

154
primeval dog howl
piercing abandonment sound
haunting recall home.

155
majority fight
over bread crumbs scattered by
elitists' nations.

156
a murder of crows
fill the air with their voices
before taking flight.

157
tenderness floats on
even hearty breezes as
dandelion seeds.

158
tranquil, clearheaded,
luminous resultant of
an oasis sleep.

159
it feels like a dream
when standing on a plateau
gazing at the sea.

160
delicate ocean
waves sooth and nourish beaches
while eroding their home.

161
sky meets earth marking
existence horizon our
azimuths of life.

162
promontories itch
a foolish conviction should
I leap I would fly.

163
when speaking truth to
power one must be primed for
state crucifixion.

164
if not vigilant
authoritarian rule
will proliferate.

165
shortsighted people
stoked on ignorance have dim
view of history.

166
pettiness leaps at
meaty opportunities
to exert itself.

167
insatiable id
requires morals to slumber
and conscious to nap.

168
unimpeachable
fundamental bloodsuckers
merit conviction.

169
avarice leeches
naked generosity
to acquire fortune.

170
shimmering sunlight
sea spray cools hot sand snapshot
eloquent beauty.

171
incessant lying
babbling obdurate forecast
fraudulent outcomes.

172
bridges of peace built
on bedrocks of beliefs span
turbulent waters.

173
democracy fails
when its citizens lose sight
of humanity.

174
canvas shoes mingle
with leather and synthetics
aboard festive deck.

175
nitpicking lucid
solutions is akin to
fanning molten steam.

176
nimble dancer sweeps
across center stage in time
to her own music.

177
crystal clear morning
dewdrops tear lavish green grass
basking in sunlight.

178
groggy morning head
cobwebs netting dream remnants
like moths in a jar.

179
butterflies are a
mournfully dwindling absence
in our modern world.

180
a summer rainstorm
thunderous memory of
relief from humidity.

181
child enters this world
offspring of expectation
nothing guaranteed.

182
depraved delinquents
poison angel minds and hearts
for devious deeds.

183
has America
reached its zenith fated to
plunge to its nadir?

184
religious abuse
methodically corrupts
healthy believers.

185
tumultuous rains
discharge from dark cloud bellies
pummel sodden earth.

186
synthesized idea
race decrees privileges
for inborn persons.

187
delusional view
lineage roots liberty
for hegemony.

188
gurgling rale of tuned
unheeded souls warning of
our bleak destiny.

189
democracy and
fair capitalism dying
from lack of freedom.

190
greed cordons workers'
rights with malice and disdain,
gluttonous ogre.

191
scoundrel seldom used
word to describe those befitting
its villainy traits.

192
oppression constant
theme resonating throughout
the wealth narrative.

193
return of southern
strategy illuminates
fraud democracy.

194
assassinations
one method power employs
to maintain control.

195
patience council's haste
on its virtues and beauty
like a seasoned monk.

196
heat radiates from
hard surfaces causing air
to dance the hula.

197
possibilities
evaporate in fiery
eruptions of time.

198
betrayal bellows
steely tirades colliding
B20 crashing cymbals.

199
dazzling gold halo
rings distant mountain range in
heraldic blue-sky.

200
bleached wan histories
render sanitized versions
of real events.

201
enemies fester
tumorous malignant boils
oozing thick dead sap.

202
high acclaim for those
sympathetic to the world's
downtrodden masses.

203
billions of dollars
spent on public elections
exclusive process.

204
biological
warfare diabolical
brainchild concoctions.

205
science lacks moral
compass seeking disclosure
wherever it leads.

206
religious zealots
claim superiority
behave like demons.

207
dancer masters form
graceful, potent, visual
vivid lithe artist.

208
ballerina still
as glass en pointe candlelight
smiles then burst to life.

209
African roots tug
at my soul proud ancestors
beckoning me home.

210
greed infects healthy
economic bodies like
the bubonic plague.

211
the adage is true
you can't save everybody
they must save themselves.

212
poetry passion
flares, illuminates chasms of
shared mortality.

213
thriving Wall Street grows
fatter as COVID-19
murders, sunders, steals.

214
saints do not reside
in the financial district
nor does compassion.

215
extreme poverty
human rights, misery twins
incessant battles.

216
an amazing word
harmony, sweet in music
and relationships.

217
bright crisp precise fugue
in D minor brass quintet
lifts me to rejoice.

218
unionized police
assault common laborers
seeking union aid.

219
enduring pursuit
eternal internal calm
accord ikigai.

220
religion used to
justify atrocities
disregards ethics.

221
fundamentalist
Christians exult themselves as
true God believers.

222
the lies begin in
earnest to re-elect a
fraud for president.

223
ultra-Christians snub
secular constitution
for bible beliefs.

224
memories float through
mind of departed sweethearts
lost potential wives.

225
drowning desire for
companionship, hermit life
nurses appealing.

226
hypocrites often
exonerate themselves while
deluding others.

227
astringent scruples
diced, Faustian transgressions
disheartened churches.

228
my heart beats strong and
steady, proud fulcrum of my
generous spirit.

229
one who serves the few
disregarding the many
egocentric breed.

230
distant passenger
jet knifes across azure sky
prods yearning for home.

231
dictatorial
reckless scofflaw president
mocks democracy.

232
cool morning stillness
tranquil earth primeval peace
glorious moment.

233
decorative chimes
offer voice to wind create
gentle placid sounds.

234
morning fog rises
mist cloud drifting above trees
zero disturbance.

235
third planet from sun
harbors corporal beings
sentient habitat.

236
first week September
fallen brittle tree leaf hints
summer departure.

237
dawn breaks from cloudy
sky, gray light illuminates
mankind awakens.

238
traffic noise bellows
cell phone junkie mesmerized
doubt he hears a thing.

239
butterflies and bees
populate backyard gardens
pollinate planet.

240
professional sports
led by black athletes demand
respect and justice.

241
morning after storm
sunshine, clear skies vaporized
rainstorm memory

242
as truth springs to light
darkness pursues to devour
its nutritious fruits.

243
tedious discourse
politics, religion, sex
exhausting exchange.

244
baked Chinook salmon
olive oil, lemon juice, zests
delicious dinner.

245
sun pours lustrous beams
bathing quiet cityscape
genesis to wane.

246
egotistical
heathen politician flouts
absence of ethics.

247
summer breezes kiss
soothes supple, hot, smooth, tanned skin
drowsy daylight dreams.

248
big brother's best friend
modern high-tech surveillance
tools of oppression.

249
rainstorm pacifies
thunder echoes in distance
quenching parched terrains.

250
speech interpreted
by brain wave-technology
sanctuary lost.

251
thick gray morning fog
gauzes quiet neighborhood
ghostly appearance.

252
high winds bring ash smell
unrestrained wildland fires near
primal fear is sparked.

253
searching for moment
of cataclysmic wisdom
before loss of faith.

254
smoke over city
incinerated forests
air sweltering hot.

255
December dawn yawns
and stretches, bleary gray eyes
give view to the day.

256
gray pall envelopes
Seattle, progeny smoke
distant forest fires.

257
cadence, verse, rhythm
imaginative language
boundless expressions.

258
nature has plans for
us, based upon stringent laws
final outcome bleak.

259
soft rain washes air
smoky gloomy shroud persists
sponge sapping sunlight.

260
glaciers breaking free
global sea level rising
Atlantis ascends.

261
wildfire tragedies
human devastation mounts
ash polluting air.

262
consumer craving
inexpensive products itch
feed oppressed labor.

263
crow knifes through smoke caws
feathers gleam in dull daylight
banks left vanishes.

264
ivory poachers
slaughter regal elephants
salacious profit.

265
shadow grazes walls
expanding, contracting shape
teasing ticklish light.

266
human predators
Bali tigers' extinction
proceed to next prey.

267
amoral creatures
financial institutions
quixotic boneyard.

268
our home galaxy
Milky Way, billions of stars
sole nest of life, Earth.

269
affection, desire
liberal, divine, carnal
tender, fervent love.

270
staunch conservatism
harbors furious racism
and subjugation.

271
hopping brown sparrow
scurrying gray squirrel halts
hawk watches from roof.

272
shorter summer days
pert bright mornings diminish
sunlight bows to night.

273
salvation path marred
condescending brash persons
distort righteous souls.

274
September wind sprints
channeled through open spaces
rustling changing leaves.

275
morning mist nestles
mundane and wonders alike
grazing light of dawn.

276
villain smoke banished
sky water purified air
welcomed rain refrain.

277
Wall Street has no heart
sole religion, profit
leech all to attain.

278
artic air stream swooshed
thrumming protective membrane
causing body chill

279
gig economy
flexible freelance worker
rarely living wage.

280
pine cones scrape concrete
pine trees fallen loins seeking
wombs to nurture seeds.

281

close my eyes, listen
steady rhythm of falling rain
calms and centers me.

282

turmoil wrought anguish
persecuted molded shapes
macabre sculptures.

283

gray squirrel nosing
on rooftop examining
gutters and downspouts.

284

color and class shape
systemic tools for fiscal
inequality.

285

sun dips blissful glow
along pale blue horizon
behind autumn trees.

286
brown spider crawls up
white wall, coaxed onto paper
set free in garden.

287
wildfire smoke returned
asthmatic atmosphere hangs
miasma of fear.

288
fall equinox past
daylight fading sleepy sun
call to hibernate.

289
Interbay District
Seattle, Washington feels
lived a lifetime here.

290
weak man wanting to
be strong, supported by weak
men's vision of strength.

291
expunged from country
Native Americans slayed
chronic genocide.

292
peace is relative
juxtaposed against conflict
earned seldom granted.

293
extermination
of societies, excuse
civilization.

294
less than one percent
indigenous people have
survived invasion.

295
prevalent sweatshops
insatiable vim demands
diluted wages.

296

voter oppression
colloquial doctrine of
colonialism.

297

one person, one vote
equal standing, deprived of
not democracy.

298

possessing a big
mouth and attitude does not
make one powerful.

299

kind people exploit
ingest their antithesis
as need arises.

300

pouring hot water
into shadow of black cup
brewing jasmine tea.

301
acoustic guitar
lithe legato melody
adrift on the wind.

302
butterscotch kisses
soft warm sticky sweet swirl of
honey and passion.

303
caramel silk skin
glistening dark amber eyes
evocative smile.

304
literature spritz
disperses word particles
entrancing mind mist.

305
poison darts pierce truth
swill lies, betrayal, deceit
deforming body.

306
rain, wind, clouds, gray, storm
form tapestry of today
glad to be indoors.

307
dawn resembles dusk
absent brilliant daylight rays
rooster's crow alarm.

308
urban garden patch
vegetables, herbs, flowers
concrete jungle farm.

309
wind and rain retreat
gray cloud blanket drain color
peaceful dark morning.

310
warm bed, cozy sleep
dreamy eyes greet solemn day
bed beckons I stay.

311
much is said today
constant barrage of voices
fewer minds listen.

312
fallen leaves reveal
abandoned bird's nest, crib to
chirping songs of life.

313
somber and sunless
tempest gray winter morning
strangles light of day.

314
shard maple tree branch
green leaves abound laid to rest
beside mailbox bank.

315
behind dark ceiling
of impenetrable clouds
cosmic stars still shine.

316
dreamed of clams and pearls
smiling women and children
at play in the sea.

317
for mind to create
poetry, stillness translates
soul oscillations.

318
wishbone convergence
two rivers meet become one
form Pittsburgh region.

319
energy smothered
under winter's frigid heart
silent darkness reigns.

320
night bear hugs morning
arctic winds chase away warmth
daylight tiptoes in.

321
floating horizon
supine dream body at rest
downy cotton peace.

322
humanity seeks
vaporizing empathy
amongst the masses.

323
threadbare darkness shrouds
urban primordial herd
modern migration.

324
ancient beliefs spear
generational progress
harpooning vision.

325
my body awakes
molded by stiffness and aches
of relentless years.

326
foul mouth gibberish
deemed authentic expression
dilutes gifted art.

327
cowards brandishing
firearms granted privileges
to intimidate.

328
breezes orchestrate
wind chimes ballet, rippling ponds
eloquent bamboo.

329
communication
riddled with redacted thoughts
is our salvation.

330
brackish tonic breeds
antagonistic bipods
foaming with hatred.

331
racist enablers
oppression peddlers decay
justice and freedom.

332
integrity too
often a human failing
chum for demon souls.

333
courageous voters
braved repressive armies to
ring liberty bell.

334
arterial rules
deterioration rips
open alloy knot.

335
dark clouds dissipate
virulent discord endures
septic residue.

336
in eye of chaos
ripened tumultuous heart
seeds find fertile soil.

337
petrichor medley
after a night of fall rain
rouses my being.

338
cold rain batters plants
satiated soil welcomes
excess drains away.

339
life umbilical
cord severed discharging soul
from earthly duties.

340
autumn grasps limpid
hands of summer and winter
transfusion altar.

341

wise mortals worship
heads bowed in solemn prayer
at foot of nature.

342

cold wind hurried down
northwest corridor chilling
exposed face and hands.

343

joyous sunlight punched
through melancholic dark clouds
proud celestial rays.

344

extinguished natives
European invasion
soulless massacre.

345

on the edge of sleep
moment of perfect stillness
meditation heart.

346
fellowship vital
sanguine ingredient in
social intercourse.

347
ship horn bellows in
the distance an echo from
my seafaring soul.

348
consumer culture
voracious reality
ethically bleak.

349
when day sounds slumber
night rain raises its voice to
sing with brother wind.

350
midday, dusk, midnight
descend on grand earth and sea
dreams whisper alone.

351
night clouds barricade
hoary moonbeams, billowy
underbelly black.

352
truth is relative
democracy is skittish
liberty observes.

353
autumnal daystar
emblazons golden stamp on
wispy blue canvas.

354
soft gray canopy
oversees nodding landscape
epoch for long sleep.

355
study handbooks for
valiant peace warriors are
scribed in blood by time.

356
fawning dependence
constitutes servitude slay
fierce autonomy.

357
plants sprouting from soil
nature whorls innate magic
disciples of fate.

358
salty tears trickled
into embryonic core
as he wept at sea.

359
mortality taps
brittle gray wrinkled temple
promising rebirth.

360
hope plea-bargains with
verity in effort to
transcend misery.

361

paper hammer, pen
chisel etch in ink on stone
tales of truth and faith.

362

autumn maple leaf
lightly brushes my bare cheek
in earthbound descent.

363

heaven records time
earth history emblazoned
eternal starlight.

364

a warm jewel smile
ignites undulating joy
essence of delight.

365

optimistic verve
sings a reverberating
melody of life.

366
firm warm embraces
construct nests of flesh and bone
placid restful home.

SUN	MON	TUE	WED	THU	FRI	SAT
	1	2	3	4	5	6
7	8	9	10	11	12	13
14	15	16	17	18	19	20
21	22	23	24	25	26	27
28	29	30				

Michael R. Lane is the author of four full-length collections of poetry: *Love & Sensuality*, *Mortal Thoughts*, *Sandbox*, and *A Drop of Midnight*.